THE END
OF THE
MIDDLE AGES

POWER AND RELIGION IN MEDIEVAL AND RENAISSANCE TIMES

THE END

OF THE

MIDDLE AGES

EDITED BY KELLY ROSCOE

Britannica®
Educational Publishing

IN ASSOCIATION WITH

ROSEN
EDUCATIONAL SERVICES

Published in 2018 by Britannica Educational Publishing (a trademark of Encyclopædia Britannica, Inc.) in association with The Rosen Publishing Group, Inc.
29 East 21st Street, New York, NY 10010

First Edition

Britannica Educational Publishing
J.E. Luebering: Executive Director, Core Editorial
Andrea R. Field: Managing Editor, Compton's by Britannica

Rosen Publishing
Meredith Day: Editor
Nelson Sá: Art Director
Brian Garvey: Designer
Cindy Reiman: Photography Manager
Bruce Donnola: Photo Researcher

Library of Congress Cataloging-in-Publication Data

Names: Roscoe, Kelly, editor.
Title: The end of the Middle Ages / edited by Kelly Roscoe.
Description: New York : Britannica Educational Publishing, 2018. | Series: Power and religion in Medieval and Renaissance times | Includes bibliographical references and index. | Audience: Grade 9 to 12.
Identifiers: LCCN 2016053739 | ISBN 9781680486230 (library bound : alk. paper)
Subjects: LCSH: Middle Ages.
Classification: LCC D203 .E527 2017 | DDC 940.1/9--dc23
LC record available at https://lccn.loc.gov/2016053739

Manufactured in China

Photo credits: Cover, pp. 3, 12, 23, 38, 54, 80, Conde/Shutterstock.com; pp. 8-9, 48-49, 77 Heritage Images/Hulton Archive/Getty Images; p. 13 Project Gutenberg (Text 10940); p. 15 Apic/ Hulton Archive/Getty Images; p. 17 Encyclopædia Britannica, Inc.; p. 21 Winchester Cathedral, Hampshire, UK/Bridgeman Images; p. 24 © Alexander/Fotolia; p. 26 © North Wind Picture Archives; pp. 28-29, 58 Photos.com/Thinkstock; pp. 30-31 © javarman/Fotolia; pp. 34-35 G. Sioen/De Agostini Picture Library/Getty Images; p. 40 Courtesy of the Burgerbibliothek, Bern; p. 44 Keystone-France/Gamma-Keystone/ Getty Images; p. 51, 82 Print Collector/Hulton Archive/Getty Images; p. 56 Courtesy of the Musée Condé, Chantilly, Fr. / photograph, Giraudon/Art Resource, New York; p. 57 Museo Civico, Bologna, Italy/Bridgeman Images; pp. 62-63 Gail Mooney/Corbis VCG/Corbis Documentary/Getty Images; p. 65 Catarina Belova/Shutterstock.com; p. 68 Private Collection/ Bridgeman Images; p. 70 Alinari-Anderson/Art Resource, New York; pp. 73, 86 Photo 12/Universal Images Group/Getty Images; p. 75 British Library, London, UK/© British Library Board. All Rights Reserved/Bridgeman Images; p. 78 Archivo Mas, Barcelona; p. 84 Courtesy of the Universitätsbibliothek, Bremen, Ger.; p. 88 Leemage/Universal Images Group/Getty Images; p. 90 DEA Picture Library/Getty Images; interior pages background and border graphics Roberto Castillo/Shutterstock.com; back cover flourish Drakonova/Shutterstock.com.

Contents

Introduction

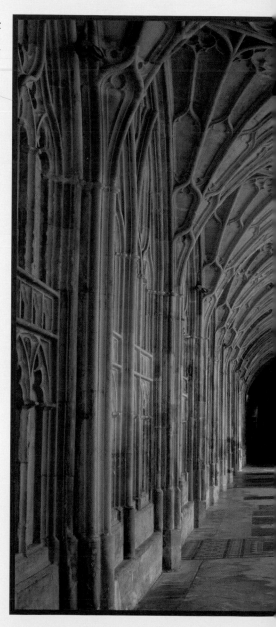

The period of European history extending from about 500 to 1400–1500 CE is traditionally known as the Middle Ages. The term was first used by 15th-century scholars to designate the period between their own time and the fall of the Western Roman Empire. The period is often considered to have its own internal divisions: early, central or high, and late. The change from ancient ways to medieval customs came so gradually, however, that it is difficult to tell exactly when the Middle Ages began. The conventional date of the beginning of the Middle Ages is 476 CE, when the Germanic general Odoacer defeated the Roman general Orestes and overthrew the emperor

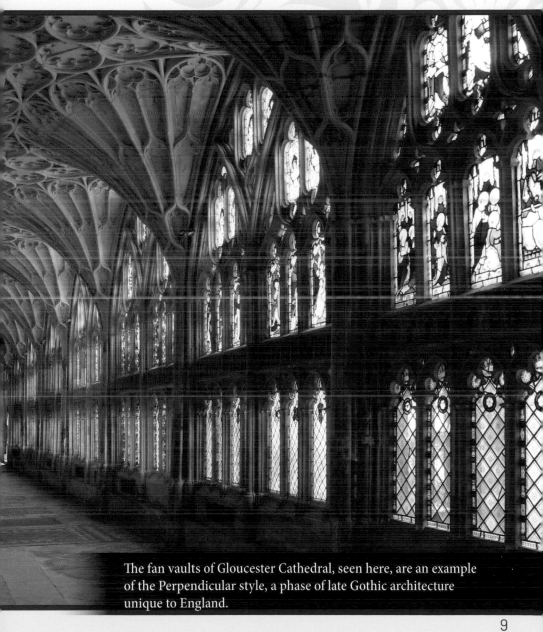

The fan vaults of Gloucester Cathedral, seen here, are an example of the Perpendicular style, a phase of late Gothic architecture unique to England.

Romulus Augustulus, ending the Western Roman Empire. (The eastern part of the empire, called the Byzantine Empire, survived for about another thousand years.) Other historians give the year 410, when Alaric, king of the Visigoths, sacked Rome. Still others say that the ancient world lasted until 750 or even 1000, when the extensive practice of slavery as in the classical world finally came to an end in western Europe.

It is equally hard to determine exactly when the Middle Ages ended, for decisive events leading to the modern age took place at different times. Historians say variously that the Middle Ages ended with the fall of Constantinople, the capital of the Byzantine Empire, in 1453; with the European "discovery" of America, in 1492; with the beginning of the Reformation, in 1517; or with the coming of the French Revolution, in 1789.

The Middle Ages was first defined as a distinct historical period in the 15th century, by scholars who saw their own time as one of great cultural progress and the revival of the Classical learning of ancient Greece and Rome. These scholars thus thought of the time between the fall of the Western Roman Empire and their own time as one of decline and then stagnation. The Middle Ages came to be seen as a long period dominated by ignorance and superstition.

Historians today, however, mostly do not accept this position. They emphasize the many important changes that occurred in society during the Middle Ages. New forms of political, social, cultural, and economic organization emerged.

The monarchies that developed laid the foundations for the nation-states of the modern period. People also first began to consider Europe as a distinct cultural unit. The Roman Catholic Church became a significant part of medieval life. Later in this period, the population began to grow greatly, agriculture and trade flourished, and cities expanded. Medieval Europe gave the world the first universities, and medieval architects produced magnificent Gothic cathedrals.

It has been traditionally held that by the 14th century the dynamic force of medieval civilization had been spent and that the late Middle Ages were characterized by decline and decay. Europe did indeed suffer disasters of war, famine, and pestilence in the 14th century, but many of the underlying social, intellectual, and political structures remained intact. In the 15th and 16th centuries, Europe experienced an intellectual and economic revival, conventionally called the Renaissance, that laid the foundation for the subsequent expansion of European culture throughout the world.

CHAPTER ONE

THE FRANKISH ASCENDANCY

Dominating present-day northern France, Belgium, and western Germany, the Germanic-speaking Franks established the most powerful Christian kingdom of early medieval western Europe. The name France (Francia) is derived from their name. The Franks emerged into recorded history in the 3rd century CE as a Germanic tribe living on the east bank of the lower Rhine River.

In 481/482 Clovis I (c. 466–511) succeeded his father, Childeric, as the ruler of the Salian Franks of Tournai. In the following years Clovis compelled the other Salian and Ripuarian tribes to submit to his authority. He then took advantage of the disintegration of the Roman Empire and led the united Franks in a series of campaigns that brought all of northern Gaul under his rule by 494. He expanded into southern Gaul, driving the Visigoths across the Pyrenees, and established a strong Frankish presence east of the Rhine. His power was recognized by the eastern emperor Anastasius, who made him a Roman consul (a high-ranking magistrate).

In the generations following the death of Clovis, the Frankish kingdom was often divided into the two kingdoms of Neustria and Austrasia, though it was occasionally reunited under Clovis's successors, the Merovingian dynasty. It was later reunited under the

King Clovis of the Franks dictates the law in the presence of his court, in a facsimile of a miniature painting from a 14th-century manuscript.

lordship and (after 751) monarchy of the eastern Frankish Arnulfing-Pippinid family (later known as the Carolingian dynasty), which included Pippin II and his successors Charles Martel, Pippin III, and Charlemagne (reigned 768–814). This dynasty brought much of western Europe under Frankish control and established diplomatic relations with Britain, Iberia, Rome, Constantinople, Christians in the Holy Land, and even Hārūn al-Rashīd, the great caliph in Baghdad.

Charlemagne and the Carolingian Dynasty

Charlemagne and his successors also patronized a vast project that they and their clerical advisers called *correctio*— restoring the fragmented western European world to an earlier idealized condition. During the Carolingian Renaissance, as it is called by modern scholars, Frankish rulers supported monastic studies and manuscript production, attempted to standardize monastic practice and rules of life, insisted on high moral and educational standards for clergy, adopted and disseminated standard versions of canon law and the liturgy, and maintained a regular network of communications throughout their dominions.

Charlemagne drew heavily on most of the kingdoms of Christian Europe, even those he conquered, for many of his advisers. Ireland sent Dicuil the geographer. The kingdoms of Anglo-Saxon England, drawn close to Rome and the Franks during the 8th century, produced the widely circulated works of Bede and the ecclesiastical reformer Boniface. Also from England was the scholar Alcuin, a product of the great school at York, who served as Charlemagne's chief adviser on ecclesiastical and other matters until becoming abbot of the monastery of St. Martin of Tours. Charlemagne's relations with the kingdoms in England remained cordial, and his political and intellectual reforms in turn shaped the development of a unified English monarchy and culture under Alfred (reigned 871–899) and his successors in the 9th and 10th centuries.

Although the Visigothic kingdom fell to Arab and Berber armies in 711, the small Christian principalities in the

This illustration from a 14th century manuscript depicts the coronation of Charlemagne on December 25, 800.

north of the Iberian Peninsula held out. They too produced remarkable scholars, some of whom were eventually judged to hold heretical beliefs. The Christological theology of adoptionism, which held that Christ in his humanity is the adopted son of God, greatly troubled the Carolingian court and generated a substantial literature on both sides before the belief was declared heterodox. But Iberia also produced scholars for Charlemagne's service, particularly Theodulf of Orleans, one of the emperor's most influential advisers.

The kingdom of the Lombards, established in northern and central Italy in the later 6th century, was originally Arian but converted to Catholic Christianity in the 7th century. Nevertheless, Lombard opposition to Byzantine forces in northern Italy and Lombard pressure on the bishops of Rome led a number of 8th-century popes to call on the assistance of the Carolingians. Pippin invaded Italy twice in the 750s, and in 774 Charlemagne conquered the Lombard kingdom and assumed its crown. Among the Lombards who migrated for a time to Charlemagne's court were the grammarian Peter of Pisa and the historian Paul the Deacon.

From 778 to 803 Charlemagne not only stabilized his rule in Frankland and Italy but also conquered and converted the Saxons and established frontier commands, or marches, at the most vulnerable edges of his territories. He built a residence for himself and his court at Aachen, which was called "a second Rome." He remained on excellent terms with the bishops of Rome, Adrian I (reigned 772–795) and Leo III (reigned 795–816). Scholars began to call Charlemagne "the father of Europe" and "the lighthouse of Europe." Although the lands under his rule were often referred to as "the kingdom of Europe," contemporaries recognized them as forming an empire, much of which extended well beyond the imperial frontiers of Rome. Because of its use in reference to the empire, the old geographical term "Europe" came to be invested with a political and cultural meaning that it did not have in Greco-Roman antiquity.

CHARLEMAGNE'S EMPIRE

Charlemagne's Kingdom
771

Increased by his conquests

PARTITION
OF VERDUN

KINGDOM
OF
LOUIS

KINGDOM
OF
CHARLES

KINGDOM OF LOTHAIR

North
Sea

Izehoe

Bremen
Verden

Elbe R.

FRISIA

Weser R.

Aller R.

SAXONY

English Channel

Utrecht

FLANDERS

Aachen

Cologne

Meuse R.

Saale R.

AUSTRASIA

Trier

Mainz

Verdun

Metz

Rhine R.

Regensburg

Danube R.

Danube R.

Theiss R.

Seine R.

Marne

Paris

BAVARIA

Salzburg

NEUSTRIA

BRITANNY

ALEMANNIA

Lech R.

Inn R.

Loire R.

Tours

Saône R.

Chalon

BURGUNDY

CARINTHIA

Drave R.

FRIULI

Save R.

ATLANTIC
OCEAN

AQUITAINE

Lyons

Rhône R.

Susa

Milan

Po R.

Verona

Bordeaux

Garonne R.

Bologna

Adriatic

GASCONY

Roncesvalles

SEPTIMANIA

PROVENCE

Pisa

Arno R.

Tiber R.

Sea

SPANISH MARCH

Narbonne

Corsica

Elba

Rome

Ebro R.

Mediterranean   Sea

The sprawling 9th-century empire of Charlemagne covered a great
part of Europe. Less than 30 years after his death, however, it was
partitioned into three weak kingdoms.

In 800 Charlemagne extracted Leo III from severe
political difficulties in Rome (Leo had been violently
attacked by relatives of the former pope and accused of various
crimes). On Christmas Day of that year Leo crowned
Charlemagne emperor of the Romans, a title that Charlemagne's
successors also adopted. Although the title gave

17

Charlemagne no resources that he did not already possess, it did not please all his subjects, and it greatly displeased the Byzantines. But it survived the Frankish monarchy and remained the most respected title of a lay ruler in Europe until the Holy Roman Empire, as it was known from the mid-12th century, was abolished by Napoleon Bonaparte in 1806, a little more than 1,000 years after Charlemagne was crowned. Historians still debate whether the coronation of 800 indicated a backward-looking last manifestation of the older world of late antiquity or a new organization of the elements of what later became Europe.

Charlemagne's kingdoms, but not the imperial title, were divided after the death of his son Louis I (the Pious) in 840 into the regions of West Francia, the Middle Kingdom, and East Francia. The last of these regions gradually assumed control over the Middle Kingdom north of the Alps. In addition, an independent kingdom of Italy survived into the late 10th century. The imperial title went to one of the rulers of these kingdoms, usually the one who could best protect Rome, until it briefly ceased to be used in the early 10th century.

CHARLEMAGNE'S LEGACY

Modern historians have noted that Charlemagne's rule had many failures: an inadequate political apparatus, the limitations of his military forces in the face of new threats from seafaring foes, the failure of his religious reforms to affect the great mass of Christians, the narrow traditionalism and clerical bias of his cultural program, and the oppressive features of his economic and social programs. Still, his effort to adjust traditional Frankish ideas of leadership and the public good to new currents in society made a crucial difference in European history. His renewal of the Roman Empire in the West provided the ideological foundation for a politically unified Europe, an idea that has inspired Europeans ever since—sometimes with unhappy consequences.

His feats as a ruler, both real and imagined, served as a standard to which many generations of European rulers looked for guidance in defining their royal functions. His religious reforms solidified the organizational structures and the liturgical practices that eventually enfolded most of Europe into a single "Church." His definition of the role of the secular authority in directing religious life laid the basis for the tension-filled interaction between temporal and spiritual authority that played a crucial role in shaping both political and religious institutions in later western European history. His cultural renaissance provided the basic tools—schools, curricula, textbooks, libraries, and teaching techniques—upon which later cultural revivals would be based. The impetus he gave to the lord-vassal relationship and to the system of agriculture known as manorialism (in which peasants held land from a lord in exchange for dues and service) played a vital role in establishing the seignorial system (in which lords exercised political and economic power over a given territory and its population). The seignorial system in turn had the potential for imposing political and social order and for stimulating economic growth. Such accomplishments certainly justify the superlatives by which he was known in his own time: *Carolus Magnus* ("Charles the Great") and *Europae pater* ("father of Europe").

CAROLINGIAN DECLINE AND ITS CONSEQUENCES

After the Carolingian dynasty died out in the male line in East Francia in 911, Conrad I, the first of a series of territorial dukes, was elected king. He was followed by a series of vigorous and ambitious rulers from the Saxon (919–1024) and Salian (1024–1125) dynasties. Otto I (reigned 936–967), the most successful of the Saxon rulers, claimed the crown of the old Lombard kingdom in Italy in 951, defeated an invading Hungarian army at the Battle of Lechfeld in 955, and was crowned emperor in Rome in 962. In contrast to the kings of East Francia, the rulers of West Francia, whose last Carolingian ruler was succeeded in 987 by the long-lasting dynasty of Hugh Capet (the Capetian dynasty), had difficulty ruling even their domains in the middle Seine valley, and they were overshadowed by the power of the territorial lords who had established themselves in principalities in the rest of the kingdom.

The end of Carolingian expansion in the early 9th century and the inability of several kings to field sufficiently large armies and reward their followers were two consequences of the division of Charlemagne's empire. In addition, the empire now shared borders with hostile peoples in the Slavic east and in the Low Countries, Scandinavia, and Iberia. The end of expansion meant that the basis of the economy shifted from mixed forest-agricultural labour and income drawn from plunder and tribute to more-intensive cultivation of lands within the kingdoms. Accordingly, kings were forced to draw on local resources to reward their followers. The consequences of these military and economic

Alfred, seen here in a stained glass from Winchester Cathedral in Hampshire, England, ruled Wessex, a Saxon kingdom in southwestern England, in the 9th century.

changes included a general weakening of royal authority, the transformation of the Carolingian aristocracy into active lords of the land, and a loss of social status for the labourers who worked the land.

In the 9th and early 10th centuries a series of invasions from Scandinavia, the lower Danube valley, and North Africa greatly weakened the Carolingian world. The divisions within the Frankish empire impaired its ability to resist the Viking and Hungarian invasions but did not destroy it. Kings and warlords ultimately either turned back the invaders, as Otto I did in 955, or absorbed them into their territories, as the kings of West Francia did with the Vikings in Normandy. In England the invasions destroyed all of the older kingdoms except Wessex, whose rulers, starting with Alfred, expanded their power until they created a single kingdom of England.

Two kinds of invaders—the Scandinavians and the Hungarians—became acculturated and Christianized during the next several centuries, creating the Christian kingdoms of Norway, Denmark, Sweden, and Hungary. Meanwhile, the Islamic world remained apart, extending from Iberia and Morocco eastward to the western edges of China and Southeast Asia.

In the case of western Europe, the attacks of the 9th and 10th centuries were the last outside invasions until the Allied landings during World War II; indeed, for a period of nearly 1,000 years western Europe was the only part of the world that was not invaded. Western Europe developed internally without outside interference, expanded geograph-ically, increased demographically, improved materially, and engaged in cultural, commercial, and technological exchanges with parallel civilizations.

CHAPTER TWO

GROWTH AND INNOVATION

lthough historians disagree about the extent of the social and material damage caused by the 9th- and 10th-century invasions, they agree that demographic growth began during the 10th century and perhaps earlier. They have also identified signs of the reorganization of lordship and agricultural labour, a process in which members of an order of experienced and determined warriors concentrated control of land in their own hands and coerced a largely free peasantry into subjection. Thus did the idea of the three orders of society—those who fight, those who pray, and those who labour—come into use to describe the results of the ascendancy of the landholding aristocracy and its clerical partners. In cooperation with bishops and ecclesiastical establishments, particularly great monastic foundations such as Cluny (established 910), the nobility of the late 11th and 12th centuries reorganized the

The abbey church of St. Peter and St. Paul at Cluny, France, was constructed between 1088 and 1130. Here the octagonal belfry tower and smaller belfry of the surviving south transept are shown.

agrarian landscape and rural society of western Europe and made it the base of urbanization, which was also well under way in the 11th century.

DEMOGRAPHIC AND AGRICULTURAL GROWTH

It has been estimated that between 1000 and 1340 the population of Europe increased from about 38.5 million people to about 73.5 million, with the greatest proportional increase occurring in northern Europe, which trebled its population. The rate of growth was not so rapid as to create a crisis of overpopulation. Rather, it was linked to increased agricultural production, which yielded a sufficient amount of food per capita, permitted the expansion of cultivated land, and enabled some of the population to become nonagricultural workers, thereby creating a new division of labour and greater economic and cultural diversity.

The late Roman countryside and its patterns of life survived well into the Carolingian period. Landlords, free peasants, half-free workers, and slaves were the main social categories. The economy was driven by cultivated fields and orchards and the use of thick forests and their products. In the late 9th century, however, political circumstances led landholders to intensify the cultivation of their lands. They did this by reducing the status of formerly free peasants to dependent servitude and by slowly elevating the status of slaves to the same dependency, creating a rural society of serfs. The old Latin word for slave, *servus*, now came to designate a category of rural workers who were not chattel

The vast majority of serfs in medieval Europe obtained their subsistence by cultivating a plot of land that was owned by a lord.

property but who were firmly bound to their lord's land. The new word for slave, *sclavus*, was derived from the source of many slaves, the Slavic lands of the east.

During the 11th and 12th centuries the chief social distinction in western European society was that between the free and the unfree. For two centuries the status of serfdom was imposed on people whose ancestors had been free and who themselves would become free only when the rise of a money economy in the late 12th century made free, rent-paying peasants more economically attractive to lords than bound serfs. The aristocracy was able to accomplish this because of weakening royal power and generosity and because of its assumption of the *bannum* ("ban"), the old public and largely royal power to command and punish (now called "banal jurisdiction"). It announced its new claims by calling them "customs" and tried them in local courts.

The aristocracy supervised the clearing of forest for the expansion of cereal cultivation but restricted the remaining forest to itself for hunting. It also forced its dependents to use its mills and local markets, to provide various labour services, and to settle more densely in the villages, which were slowly coordinated with an expanded system of parishes (local churches with lay patrons, to which peasants had to pay the tithe, or one-tenth of their produce). Serfdom was gradually eliminated in western Europe during the 13th and 14th centuries as a result of economic changes that made agricultural labour less financially advantageous to lords. During the same period, however, serfdom increased in eastern Europe, where it lasted until the 19th century.

The new stratification of society into the categories of free and unfree was accompanied by the transformation of the late Carolingian aristocratic family from a widespread association of both paternal and maternal relatives to a narrower lineage, in which paternal ancestry and paternal control of the disposition of inheritance dominated. Family memory restricted itself to a founding paternal ancestor, ignoring the line of maternal ancestors, and the new lineages

The first medieval knights were professional cavalry warriors, and the process of entering knighthood often became formalized.

identified themselves with a principal piece of property, from which they often took a family name. They also patronized religious establishments, which memorialized the families in prayers, enhanced their local prestige, and often provided them burial in their precincts.

The new lords of the land identified themselves primarily as warriors. Because new technologies of warfare, including heavy cavalry, were expensive, fighting men required substantial material resources as well as considerable leisure to train. The economic and political transformation of the countryside filled these two needs. The old armies of free men of different levels of wealth were replaced by new armies of specialist knights. The term "knight" (Latin *miles*) came into more frequent use to designate anyone who could satisfy the new military requirements, which included the wealthiest and most powerful lords as well as fighting men from far lower levels of society. The new order gradually developed its own spirit, reflected in the ideal of chivalry, the knight's code of conduct. The distinction between free and unfree was reinforced by the distinction between those who fought, even at the lowest level, and those who could not. Those who functioned at the lowest level of military service worked hard to distinguish themselves from those who laboured in the fields.

Technological Innovations

The increases in population and agricultural productivity were accompanied by a technological revolution that introduced new sources of power and a cultural "machine-mindedness," both of which were incorporated into a wide spectrum of economic enterprises. The chief new sources of power were the horse, the water mill, and the windmill. Europeans began to breed both the specialized warhorse, which mounted warriors would ride with stirrups to provide a better seat and greater striking force, and the draft horse, now shod with iron horseshoes that protected the hooves from the damp clay soils of northern Europe. The draft horse was faster and more efficient than the ox, the traditional beast of burden. The invention of the new horse collar in the 10th century, a device that pulled from the horse's shoulders rather than from its neck and windpipe, immeasurably increased the animal's pulling power.

The extensive network of rivers in western Europe spurred the development of the water mill, not only for grinding grain into flour but also by the 12th century for converting simple rotary motion into reciprocal motion. Where water was not readily available, Europeans constructed windmills, which had been imported from the Middle East, thereby spreading the mill to even more remote locations.

In heavily forested and mountainous parts of western Europe, foresters, charcoal burners, and miners formed sep-

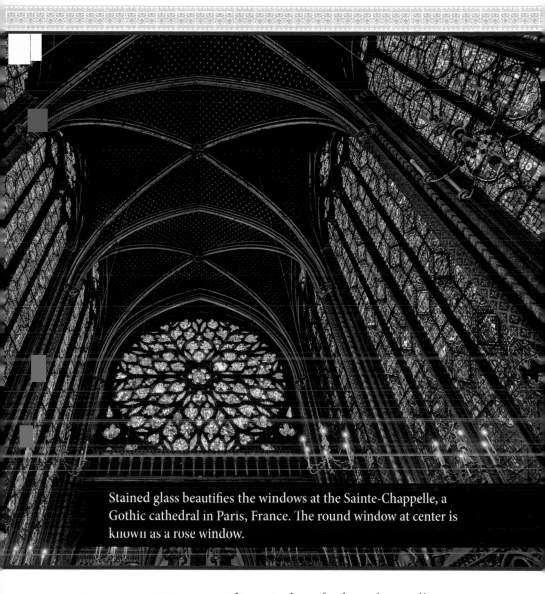

Stained glass beautifies the windows at the Sainte-Chappelle, a Gothic cathedral in Paris, France. The round window at center is known as a rose window.

arate communities, providing timber, fuel, and metallic ores in abundance. The demands of domestic and public building and shipbuilding threatened to deforest much of Europe as early as the 13th century. Increasingly refined metallurgical technology produced not only well-tempered swords, daggers, and armour for warriors but also elaborate domestic

GOTHIC ARCHITECTURE

Architecture was the most important and original art form during the Gothic period (the mid-12th century to as late as the end of the 16th century in some areas). The principal structural characteristics of Gothic architecture arose out of medieval masons' efforts to solve the problems associated with supporting heavy masonry ceiling vaults over wide spans. The problem was that the heavy stonework of the traditional arched barrel vault and the groin vault exerted a tremendous downward and outward pressure that tended to push the walls upon which the vault rested outward, thus collapsing them. A building's vertical supporting walls thus had to be made extremely thick and heavy in order to contain the barrel vault's outward thrust.

Medieval masons solved this difficult problem about 1120 with a number of brilliant innovations. First and foremost they developed a ribbed vault, in which arching and intersecting stone ribs support a vaulted ceiling surface that is composed of mere thin stone panels. This greatly reduced the weight (and thus the outward thrust) of the ceiling vault, and since the vault's weight was now carried at discrete points (the ribs) rather than along a continuous wall edge, separate widely spaced vertical piers to support the ribs could replace the continuous thick walls. The round arches of the barrel vault were replaced by pointed (Gothic) arches, which distributed thrust in more directions downward from the topmost point of the arch.

Since the combination of ribs and piers relieved the intervening vertical wall spaces of their supportive function, these walls could be built thinner and could even be opened up with large windows or other glazing. A crucial point was that the outward thrust of the ribbed ceiling vaults was carried across the outside walls of the nave, first to an attached outer buttress and then to a freestanding pier by means of a half arch known as a flying buttress. The flying buttress leaned against the upper exterior of the nave (thus counteracting the vault's outward thrust), crossed over the low side aisles of the nave, and terminated in the freestanding buttress pier, which ultimately absorbed the ceiling vault's thrust.

These elements enabled Gothic masons to build much larger and taller buildings than their Romanesque predecessors and to give their structures more complicated ground plans. The skillful use of flying buttresses made it possible to build extremely tall, thin-walled buildings whose interior structural system of columnar piers and ribs reinforced an impression of soaring verticality.

ware. Glazed pottery and glass also appeared even in humble homes, which were increasingly built of stone rather than wood and thatch.

The most striking and familiar examples of the technological revolution are the great Gothic cathedrals and other churches, which were constructed from the 12th century onward. Universally admired for their soaring height and stained-glass windows, they required mathematically precise designs; considerable understanding of the properties of subsoils, stone, and timber; near-professional architectural skills; complex financial planning; and a skilled labour force. They are generally regarded as the most-accomplished engineering feats of the Middle Ages.

Urban Growth

The experience of building great churches was replicated in the development of the material fabric of the new and expanded cities. The cities of the Carolingian world were few and small. Their functions were limited to serving the needs of the kings, bishops, or monasteries that inhabited them. Some, especially those that were close to the Mediterranean, were reconfigured Roman cities. In the north a Roman nucleus sometimes became the core of a new city, but just as often cities emerged because of the needs of their lords. The northern cities were established as local market centres and then developed into centres of diversified artisanal production with growing merchant populations. In the 10th and 11th centuries new cities were founded and existing cities increased in area and population. They were usually enclosed within a wall once their inhabitants thought that the city had reached the limits of its expansion. As populations grew and suburbs began to surround the walls, many cities built new and larger walls to enclose the new space. The succession of concentric rings of town walls offers a history of urban growth in many cities. Inhabitants also took pride in their city's appearance, as evidenced by the elaborate decorations on city gates, fountains, town halls (in northern Italy from the 10th century), and other

Carcassonne is a fortified city in the south of France that was restored by architect Eugène Viollet-le-Duc in the late 19th century. Its first fortifications date from the pre-Roman period.

public spaces. Cities were cultural as well as economic and political centres, and their decoration was as important to their inhabitants as their water systems, defenses, and marketplaces.

The cities attracted people from the countryside, where the increasing productivity of the farms was freeing many peasants from working on the land. Various mercantile and craft guilds were formed beginning in the 10th century to protect their members' common interests. The merchants' guilds and other associations also contributed to the emergence of the sworn commune, or the self-regulating city government, originally chartered by a bishop, count, or king. The city distinguished itself from the countryside, even as it extended its influence there. During the 12th century this distinction was recognized culturally, when the Latin word *urbanitas* ("urbanity") came to be applied to the idea of acceptable manners and informed Christian belief, while *rusticitas* ("rusticity") came to mean inelegance and backwardness. Despite this awareness, cities had to protect their food supplies and their trade and communication routes, and thus in both southern and northern Europe the city and its *contado* (region surrounding the city) became closely linked.

In some areas of northern Europe, particular kinds of manufacturing became prominent, especially dyeing, weaving, and finishing woolen cloth. Wool production was the economic enterprise in which the cities of the southern Low Countries took pride of place, and other cities developed elaborate manufacturing of metalwork and armaments. Still others became market centres of essential products that could not be produced locally, such as wine. This specialized production led to the proliferation of long-range trade and the creation of communications networks along the rivers of western Europe, where many cities were located. Although some lords, including the kings of England, were reluctant to recognize the towns' autonomy, most eventually agreed that the rapidly increasing value of the towns as centres of manufacturing and trade was worth the risk of their practical independence.

Originally a product of the agrarian dynamic that shaped society after the year 1000, the growing towns of western Europe became increasingly important, and their citizens acquired great wealth, usually in cooperation rather than conflict with their rulers. The towns helped transform the agrarian world out of which they were originally created into a precapitalist manufacturing and market economy that influenced both urban and rural development.

CHAPTER THREE

REFORM AND RENEWAL

A number of the movements for ecclesiastical reform that emerged in the 11th century attempted to sharpen the distinction between clerical and lay status. Most of these movements drew upon the older Christian ideas of spiritual renewal and reform, which were thought necessary because of the degenerative effects of the passage of time on fallen human nature. They also drew upon standards of monastic conduct, especially those regarding celibacy and devotional rigour, that had been articulated during the Carolingian period and were now extended to all clergy, regular (monks) and secular (priests).

ECCLESIASTICAL REFORM

Virginity, long seen by Christian thinkers as an equivalent to martyrdom, was now required of all clergy. It has been argued that the requirement of celibacy was established to protect ecclesiastical property, which had greatly increased, from being alienated by the clergy or from becoming the basis of dynastic power. The doctrine of clerical celibacy and freedom from sexual pollution was one of the bases of the reform movement that took shape during this period. Other important ideas included the notion that the clergy should not be dependent on the laity, and the insistence on the *libertas* ("liberty") of the church—the freedom to accomplish its divinely ordained mission without interference from any secular authority. Most of these reform movements originated in reforming monasteries in transalpine Europe, which cooperative lay patrons and supporters protected from predatory violence.

By the middle of the 11th century, the reform movements reached Rome itself, when the emperor Henry III intervened in a schism that involved three claimants to the papal throne. At the Synod of Sutri in 1046 he appointed a transalpine candidate of his own   Suidger, archbishop of Bamberg, who became Pope Clement II (1046–47)—and removed the papal office from the influence of the local Roman nobility, which had largely controlled it since the 10th century. A series of popes, including Leo IX (1049–54) and Urban II (1088–99), promoted what is known as Gregorian Reform, named for its most zealous proponent, Pope Gregory VII (1073–85). They urged reform throughout Europe by means of their official correspondence and their sponsorship of regional church councils. They also restructured the hierarchy, placing the papal office at the head of reform efforts and articulating a systematic claim to papal authority over clergy and, in very many matters, over laity as well.

In this 11th-century codex, Leo IX (*left*) consecrates the rebuilt monastery church of St.-Arnould-de-Metz, which is being offered to him by Abbot Warinus of Metz.

The emotional intensity of ecclesiastical reform led to outbursts of religious enthusiasm from both supporters and opponents. Many laypeople also enthusiastically supported reform; indeed, their support was a key factor in its ultimate success. The increase in lay piety on the side of reform was indicated by the events of 1095, when Urban II called on lay warriors to cease preying on the weak and on each other and to undertake the liberation of the Holy Land from its Muslim conquerors and occupiers. The enormous military expedition that captured Jerusalem in 1099 and established for a century the Latin kingdom of Jerusalem, an expedition only much later called the First Crusade, is as dramatic a sign as possible of the vitality and devotion of clerical and lay reformers.

The reform movement had a pronounced effect on church and society. It produced an independent clerical order, hierarchically organized under the popes. The clergy claimed both a teaching authority (magisterium) and a disciplinary authority, based on theology and canon law, that defined orthodoxy and heterodoxy and regulated much of lay and all of clerical life. The clergy also expressed its

THE COUNCIL OF CLERMONT

The Council of Clermont convoked by Pope Urban II on November 18, 1095, was attended largely by bishops of southern France as well as a few representatives from northern France and elsewhere. Much important ecclesiastical business was transacted, which resulted in a series of canons, among them one that renewed the Peace of God and another that granted a full indulgence (the remission of all penance for sin) to those who undertook to aid Christians in the East. Then in a great outdoor assembly the pope, a Frenchman, addressed a large crowd.

His exact words will never be known, since the only surviving accounts of his speech were written years later, but he apparently stressed the plight of Eastern Christians, the molestation of pilgrims, and the desecration of the holy places. He urged those who were guilty of disturbing the peace to turn their warlike energies toward a holy cause. He emphasized the need for penance along with the acceptance of suffering and taught that no one should undertake this pilgrimage for any but the most exalted of motives.

The response was immediate and overwhelming, probably far greater than Urban had anticipated. Cries of "Deus le volt" ("God wills it") were heard everywhere, and it was decided that those who agreed to go should wear a cross. Moreover, it was not only warrior knights who responded; a popular element, apparently unexpected and probably not desired, also came forward.

The era of Clermont witnessed the concurrence of three significant developments: First, there existed as never before a popular religious fervour that was not without marked eschatological tendencies in which the holy city of Jerusalem figured prominently. Second, war against the infidel had come to be regarded as a religious undertaking, a work pleasing to God. Finally, western Europe now possessed the ecclesiastical and secular institutional and organizational capacity to plan such an enterprise and carry it through.

authority through a series of energetic church councils, from the first Lateran Council in 1123 to the fourth Lateran Council in 1215, and greatly enhanced both the ritual and legal authority of the popes.

THE FIRST CRUSADE

Following Pope Urban's speech, preparations began in both East and West. Alexius, the Byzantine emperor, who had doubtless anticipated the mustering of some sort of auxiliary force, apparently soon realized that he would have to provide for and police a much larger influx of warriors. In the West, as the leaders began to assemble their armies, those who took the cross sought to raise money, often by selling or mortgaging property, both for the immediate purchase of equipment and for the long-term needs of the journey.

PREPARATIONS FOR THE CRUSADE

As preparations were under way, several less-organized bands of knights and peasants, commonly known as the "People's Crusade," set out across Europe. One of these groups was led by the notorious Count Emicho and was responsible for a series of pogroms, or massacres, of Jews in several Rhenish towns in 1096. Traditionally recognized as an important turning point in Jewish and Christian relations in the Middle Ages—in fact, it is often cited as a pivotal moment in the history of anti-Semitism—these attacks occurred first in Speyer and then with increasing ferocity in Worms, Mainz, and Cologne. The Jews of these towns often sought, and sometimes received, the protection of the bishop or futilely took refuge in local homes and temples. Forced by the Crusaders to convert or die, many Jews chose death. There are accounts of Jews committing suicide and even killing their children rather than converting or submitting to execution by the Crusaders. Though zealotry of this nature is not unique to Christianity, these massacres did not go unnoticed even by fellow Christians. Indeed, some contemporary Christian accounts attributed the defeat of the People's Crusade to them. After the massacres, the Crusaders moved on to Hungary, where they were routed by the Hungarian king and suffered heavy losses. Emicho, who may not have participated in all the pogroms, escaped and returned home in disgrace.

The main Crusading force, which departed in August 1096 as Urban directed, consisted of four major contingents. Godfrey of Bouillon, leader of the first large army to depart and duke of Lower Lorraine since 1087, was the only major prince from the German kingdom involved in the Crusade, though he and his associates largely spoke French. Joined by his brothers, Eustace and Baldwin, and a kinsman, Baldwin of Le Bourcq, Godfrey took the land route and crossed Hungary without incident. Markets and provisions were supplied in Byzantine territory, and, except for some pillaging, the army reached Constantinople without serious problems on December 23, 1096.

A second force was organized by Bohemond, a Norman from southern Italy. The third and largest army was assembled by Raymond of Saint-Gilles, the count of Toulouse. He was accompanied by Adhémar, bishop of Le Puy, whom the pope had named as legate for the Crusade.

xb. cime iour dou mois li uaillans

Godfrey of Bouillon led one of the main armies of the First Crusade, reaching Constantinople in only a few months.

Raymond led his followers, including a number of noncombatant pilgrims whom he supported at his own expense, across northern Italy, around the head of the Adriatic Sea, and then southward into Byzantine territory. This large body caused considerable trouble in Dalmatia and clashed with Byzantine troops as it approached the capital, where Raymond arrived on April 21. Meanwhile, the fourth army, under Robert of Flanders, had crossed the Adriatic from Brindisi. No king took part in the First Crusade, and the predominantly French-speaking participants came to be known by the Muslims as Franks.

The presence near Constantinople of massive military forces, numbering perhaps 4,000 mounted knights and 25,000 infantry, posed a serious problem for Alexius, and there was occasional disorder. Forced to consider imperial interests, which, it soon became evident, were different from the objective of the Crusaders, the emperor required each Crusade leader to promise under oath to restore to him any conquered territory that had belonged to the empire before the Turkish invasions and to swear loyalty to him while the Crusaders remained in his domain. Since there was never any plan for the Crusade to go beyond the far-flung borders of the old Roman Empire, this would effectively give all conquests to the emperor. Only Bohemond willingly took the emperor's oath. The others did so under duress, and Raymond swore only a lukewarm oath to respect the property and person of the emperor. Despite this, Raymond and Alexius became good friends, and Raymond remained the strongest defender of the emperor's rights throughout the Crusade.

FROM CONSTANTINOPLE TO ANTIOCH

Late in May 1097 the Crusaders and a contingent of Byzantine soldiers reached the capital of the Turkish sultanate, Nicaea (now İznik, Turkey), which surrendered to the Byzantines on June 19. The Crusade army left Nicaea for Antioch on June 26 and found crossing the arid and mountainous Anatolia difficult. At Dorylaeum on July 1, 1097, Turks attacked the advance column of the Crusader army. Despite the heat and a rain of arrows, the Crusaders held their ground, and, when the rest of the army drew up, the Turks were routed. A major victory in open warfare had been achieved by cooperation between the separate Western contingents and the Greeks.

Further advance across Anatolia was even more arduous, and it was only after suffering many casualties, especially in the region of the Taurus Mountains, that the Crusaders arrived near Antioch on October 20. Meanwhile, Godfrey's brother Baldwin left the main army to involve himself in Armenian politics and then became ruler of Edessa. The first of the Crusader states, the county of Edessa would provide a valuable buffer against Turkish attacks on Antioch and other Christian territories.

One of the great cities of the Levant and one of the patriarchal sees of Christianity, Antioch was surrounded by an enormous circle of walls studded with more than 400 towers. Despite reinforcements and supplies from Genoese and English ships and later from the patriarch of Jerusalem, then in Cyprus, the siege proved long and difficult, and many died of starvation or disease. Spring brought the threat of counterattack by a relief force under Kerbogha of Mosul. The situation seemed so hopeless that some Crusaders deserted and attempted to return home. Among these was Peter the Hermit, who was caught and returned to the host, where he was quietly forgiven. Another deserter was the French knight Stephen of Blois, who was cut off from the main body of the army by Kerbogha's forces and judged, not unreasonably, that the Crusaders were doomed. On his way home Stephen met Alexius, who was marching at the head of a Byzantine relief force, and convinced him that Antioch's cause was hopeless. The emperor's decision to turn back, however justified tactically, was a diplomatic blunder; when the Crusaders learned of the emperor's move, they felt free from any obligation to return the city to him.

Bohemond, meanwhile, proposed that the first to enter the city should have possession of it, provided the emperor did not make an appearance. The Norman had, in fact, already made contact with a discontented commander within, who proceeded to admit him over a section of the walls on June 3, 1098. The other Crusaders followed Bohemond into the dozing city and quickly captured it. Only the citadel held out.

Thus, Antioch was restored to Christian rule. The victory, however, was incomplete. Kerbogha arrived with an enormous Turkish army and completely invested the city, which was already very low on provisions. Once again the situation seemed hopeless. Disagreements between the leaders persisted and were accentuated by arguments over the validity of what had come to be called the Holy Lance, which a Provençal priest found below the cathedral and insisted was the lance that, according to the Gospels, had pierced the side of Jesus Christ when he hung on the cross. Nonetheless, on June 28 the Crusader army moved out of the city. The Turkish forces were not of high quality and had only tenuous loyalty to Kerbogha. When they saw the size of the Crusade forces and the resolve of the men, the Turks began to flee. With the evaporation of Kerbogha's army, the citadel finally surrendered to Bohemond, and its garrison was permitted to leave. Rejoicing was tempered by a devastating epidemic that took many lives, including that of the legate, Adhémar of Le Puy, who, as the spiritual leader of the Crusade, had been a wise counselor and a stabilizing influence whom the leaders could ill afford to lose.

The Crusade leaders then fell into violent disagreement over the final disposition of Antioch. Bohemond, who had been responsible for the capture of the city and then had led its defense, wanted it for himself. Raymond, however, insisted that it be returned to the emperor. Unable to come to terms on Antioch, Bohemond and Raymond refused to march to Jerusalem, which effectively stalled the Crusade. The leaders agreed to depart only after the rank and file threatened to tear down the walls of Antioch. On January 13, 1099, the army then set out for Jerusalem under the leadership of Raymond of Saint-Gilles. As they moved south, Tancred and Robert of Normandy and, later, Godfrey and Robert of Flanders joined them. Bohemond, ignoring his previous oaths, remained in Antioch.

THE SIEGE OF JERUSALEM

Not far from Beirut, the army entered the territory of the Fāṭimid caliphs of Cairo, who, as Shīʿite Muslims, were enemies of the Sunnite Seljuqs and the caliphs of Baghdad. In August 1098 the Fāṭimids had occupied Jerusalem. The final drive of the First Crusade, therefore, was against the Fāṭimids of Egypt, not the Seljuqs.

The siege of Jerusalem, seen in this 15th-century miniature, was a remarkable victory by the Christians that inspired later Crusades.

On June 7, 1099, the Christian army—by then considerably reduced to perhaps 1,200–1,500 cavalry and 12,000 foot soldiers—encamped before Jerusalem, whose governor was well supplied and confident that he could withstand a siege until a relief force arrived from Egypt. The Crusaders, on the other hand, were short of supplies and would be until six vessels arrived at Jaffa (Yafo) and managed to unload before the port was blockaded by an Egyptian squadron. On July 8 a strict fast was ordered, and, with the Muslims scoffing from the walls, the entire army, preceded by the clergy, marched in solemn procession around the city, thence to the Mount of Olives, where Peter the Hermit preached with his former eloquence.

Siege towers were carried up to the walls on July 13–14, and on July 15 Godfrey's men took a sector of the walls, and others followed on scaling ladders. When the nearest gate was opened, Tancred and Raymond entered, and the Muslim governor surrendered to the latter in the Tower of David. The governor, along with his bodyguard, was escorted out of the city. Tancred promised protection in the Aqṣā Mosque, but his orders were disobeyed. Hundreds of men, women, and children, both Muslim and Jewish, perished in the general slaughter that followed.

The Crusaders, therefore, attained their goal three long years after they had set out. Against the odds this struggling, fractious, and naive enterprise had made its way from western Europe to the Middle East and conquered two of the best-defended cities of the time. From a modern perspective, the improbability of the First Crusade's success is staggering. For medieval men and women, though, the agent of victory was God himself, who worked miracle after miracle for his

uenir ypxent:

During the Second Crusade in the summer of 1148, the Crusaders attempted to besiege the city of Damascus, but they were forced to retreat after only four days.

faithful knights. It was this firm belief that would sustain centuries of Crusading.

The First Crusade had other, unintended effects. The success of Genoa, Pisa, and other Italian maritime cities in supplying the Christian outposts in the Holy Land increased their already considerable wealth and political power, which were soon comparable to that of Venice. Proposals for later

Crusades often led to searching analyses, not only of specific military, financial, and logistical requirements but also of the social reforms that such ventures would require in the kingdoms of Europe. Finally, by bringing Latin Christians other than pilgrims deeper into western Eurasia than they had ever been before, the Crusade movement led Europeans in the 12th century to a greater interest in distant parts of the world.

The Papacy and the Holy Roman Empire

The reform movement also erupted in a violent conflict, known as the Investiture Controversy, between Gregory VII and the emperor Henry IV (reigned 1056–1105/06). In this struggle the pope claimed extraordinary authority to correct the emperor; he twice declared the emperor deposed before Henry forced him to flee Rome to Salerno, where he died in exile. Despite Gregory's apparent defeat, the conflicts undermined imperial claims to authority and shattered the Carolingian-Ottonian image of the emperor as the lay equal of the bishop of Rome, responsible for acting in worldly matters to protect the church. The emperor, like any other layman, was now subordinate to the moral discipline of churchmen.

Some later emperors, notably the members of the Hohenstaufen dynasty—including Frederick I Barbarossa (1152–90), his son Henry VI (1190–97), and his grandson Frederick II (1220–50)—reasserted modified claims for imperial authority and intervened in Italy with some success. But Barbarossa's political ambitions were thwarted by the northern Italian cities of the Lombard League and the forces of Pope Alexander III at the Battle of Legnano in 1176. Both Henry VI and Frederick II, who had united the imperial and Lombard crowns and added to them that of the rich and powerful Norman kingdom of Sicily, faced similar resistance. Frederick himself was deposed by Pope Innocent IV in 1245. Succession disputes following Frederick's death and that of his immediate successors led to the Great Interregnum of 1250–73, when no candidate received enough electoral votes to become emperor. The interregnum ended only with the election of the Habsburg ruler Rudolf I (1273–91), which resulted in the increasing provincialization of the imperial office in favour of Habsburg dynastic and territorial interests. In 1356 the Luxembourg emperor Charles IV (1316–78) issued the Golden Bull, which established the number of imperial electors at seven (three ecclesiastical and four lay princes) and articulated their powers.

Although the emperor possessed the most prestigious of all lay titles, the actual authority of his office was very limited. Both the Habsburgs and their rivals used the office to promote their dynastic self-interests until the Habsburg line ascended the throne permanently with the reign of Frederick III (1442–93), the last emperor to be crowned in Rome. The imperial office and title were abolished when Napoleon dissolved the Holy Roman Empire in 1806.

CHAPTER FOUR

THE
CONSEQUENCES OF
REFORM

he conflicts between emperors and popes constituted one conspicuous result of the reform movement. Other important results were the transformation and new institutionalization of learning, the reconstitution of the church, the intensification of ecclesiastical discipline, and the growth of territorial monarchies. Each of these developments was supported by the agricultural, technological, and commercial expansion of the 10th and 11th centuries.

THE TRANSFORMATION OF THOUGHT AND LEARNING

The arguments of the papal-imperial debate revealed the importance of establishing a set of canonical texts on the basis of which both sides could argue. A number of academic disciplines, particularly the study of dialectic, had developed considerably between the 9th and 12th centuries. By the 12th century it had become the most widely studied intellectual discipline, in part because it was an effective tool for constructing and refuting arguments. The Gregorian reformers had also based their arguments on canon law, and a number of Gregorian and post-Gregorian collections, particularly that of Ivo of Chartres (c. 1040–1116), pointed the way toward the creation of a commonly accessible canon law. That goal was achieved in about 1140–50 in two successive versions (perhaps by two different authors) of a lawbook called *Concordia discordantium canonum* ("Concordance of Discordant Canons"), or *Decretum*, attributed to Master Gratian. The *Decretum* became the standard introductory text of ecclesiastical law. Simultaneously, the full text of the 6th-century body of Roman law, later called the *Corpus Iuris Civilis* ("Body of Civil Law"), began to circulate in northern Italy and was taught in the schools of Bologna. The learned character of the revived Roman law contributed powerfully to the development of legal science throughout Europe in the following centuries.

Early in the 12th century, Hugh of Saint-Victor (1096–1141), schoolmaster of a house of canons just outside Paris, wrote a description of all the subjects of learning, the *Didascalicon*. Hugh's contemporary, Peter Abelard (1079–1142), taught dialectic at Paris to crowds of students, many of whom became high officials in ecclesiastical and secular institutions. The teaching methods of scholars such as Gratian, Hugh, Abelard, and others became the foundation of Scholasticism, the method used by the new schools in the teaching of arts, law, medicine, and theology. In theology

This 14th-century miniature portrait by Jean de Meun of Peter Abelard and Héloïse hangs in the Musée Condé, Chantilly, France.

itself, comparable canonical work was done by Peter Lombard (c. 1100–60) in his *Sententiarum libri iv* ("Four Books of Sentences"), which became, next to the Bible, the fundamental teaching text of theology.

But not all Christians admired the new Scholastic theology. The Scholastic teaching of Scripture replaced the early contemplative monastic style of explanation with dialectical investigative techniques and speculative theology. Many monks and some outraged laity thought that Scripture was being mishandled, stripped of its dignity and mystery in the service of feeble human logic and cold rationality. They did not, however, stop the tide, as Scholastic theology created a complex, effective, and highly persuasive means of discussing both the complexities of divinity and the moral obligations of Christians on earth.

As groups of teachers organized themselves into guilds in the late 12th and early 13th centuries, they and their students received imperial, papal, and royal privileges. About 1200 these associations, modeling themselves on ecclesiastical corporations, developed into the first universities. During the remainder of the 13th century, clerical teaching authority within the universities was articulated. The first guilds were formed for the teaching of law at several schools in Bologna and for the teaching of arts and theology at Paris and later at Oxford, Cambridge, and other towns. With the foundation of the University of Prague in 1348, the model crossed the Rhine River for the first time. By the 15th century it had become a standard fixture of European learning.

University teachers insisted on the right to define teaching authority. Proclaiming the earliest version of academic freedom, they rejected outside interference and asserted that their professional competence alone entitled them to determine the content of disciplines and the

The University of Bologna became in the 12th and 13th centuries the principal centre for studies in civil and canon law. This sculpture of students is from the tomb of Giovanni da Legnano, a canon lawyer there.

Apotheosis of St. Thomas Aquinas is an altarpiece by Francesco Traini, 1363, in Santa Caterina, Pisa, Italy.

standards for admitting, examining, graduating, and certifying students. They also transformed both the written script and the nature of the material book. Since teaching required a readable script and books whose texts were as close to identical as possible, the distinctive "Gothic" or "black letter" script was developed, which standardized abbreviations and the writing style used in texts.

The presence of universities of teachers and students in western European society was significant in itself. The universities reflected favourably on the cities in which they were located and on the rulers who protected them. The rulers also benefited from the opportunity to recruit increasingly educated public servants and bureaucrats from these institutions. The church benefited too, since the universities produced theologians, canon lawyers, and other officials that the church—even the papal office—now seemed to require.

The universities aided in the recovery and dissemination of Aristotelianism, particularly in the physical sciences and metaphysics. Only the new universities, moreover, could have housed and spread the intellectual work of Thomas Aquinas (1224/25–1274) and Bonaventure (1217–74), the greatest theologians of the 13th century, and of Henry of Segusio (Hostiensis; c. 1200–71) and Sinibaldo Fieschi (later Pope Innocent IV, reigned 1243–54), the greatest canon lawyers of the century.

PAPAL ADMINISTRATION

In the 12th century, the organization of the universal church and local churches acquired a symmetry and consistency. Members of the clergy were ranked in terms of sacramental orders, minor and major. When a boy or young man entered the clergy, he received the tonsure, symbolizing his new status. He might then move in stages through the minor orders: acolyte, exorcist, lector, and doorkeeper. At the highest of minor orders the candidate could still leave the clergy. Many clerics in minor orders served in the administration of secular and ecclesiastical institutions. They also sometimes caused trouble in secular society, since even they received benefit of clergy, or exemption from trial in secular courts. Ordination to the major orders—subdeacon (elevated to a major order by Pope Innocent III in 1215), deacon, and priest—entailed vows of chastity and conferred sacramental powers on the recipient.

At the head of the Latin Christian church was the pope, whose powers were now articulated in canon law, most of which was made by the popes themselves and by their legal advisers. Not only did popes claim powers over even secular rulers in many instances, but a number of rulers, including King John of England (reigned 1199–1216), submitted their kingdoms to the popes and received them back to govern for their new spiritual and temporal masters. The popes also issued charters of foundation for universities, convened church councils, called Crusades and commissioned preachers to deliver Crusade sermons, and appointed papal judges delegate or subdelegate to investigate specific problems. In all these areas, as in the articulation of canon law, papal authority directly affected the lives of all Christians, as well as the lives of Jews and Muslims in their relations with Christians.

The popes were assisted by the College of Cardinals, which was transformed during the papal-imperial conflict from a group of Roman liturgical assistants into a body of advisers individually appointed by the popes. Among its duties articulated in conciliar and papal decrees of 1059 and 1179—rules still in effect in the Roman Catholic Church today—was to elect the pope. A cardinal could be a cardinal bishop (if the church he was given was outside the city of Rome, whose only bishop, of course, was the pope himself), a cardinal priest, or a cardinal deacon. Cardinals also had different roles. The cardinal bishop of Ostia, for example, always crowned a new pope. For some time the senior cardinal deacon gave the pope his papal name, a practice that began in the 10th century, perhaps in imitation of monastic tradition.

The papacy developed other means to implement its authority. After the Concordat of Worms (1122), which settled some aspects of the Investiture Controversy, popes held regular assemblies of higher clergy in church councils, the first of which was the first Lateran Council in 1123. Conciliar legislation was the means by which reform principles

The abdication of Henry IV in favour of son Henry V is depicted in this detail from the *Chronicle of Ekkehard von Aura*, 12th century.

were most efficiently formulated and disseminated to the highest clerical levels. Although the
popes controlled councils in the 12th, 13th, and
14th centuries, later councils sometimes opposed
papal authority with claims to conciliar authority,
a position generally known as conciliarism. Papal
legates, judges, and emissaries, widely used by
Gregory VII and later popes, were dispatched
with full papal authority to deal with issues in distant parts of Europe.

Papal collectors, who received funds owed
to the popes for Crusading or other purposes, were
also essential components of papal government.
The papal chamberlain of Celestine III (1191–98),
Cencio Savelli (later Pope Honorius III; 1216–27),
produced the *Liber Censuum* ("The Book of the Cen-
sus") in 1192, the first comprehensive account of
the sources of papal funding. In this respect, as in
the formal communications of the papal chancery,
the pope created an influential model, imitated by
all other European principalities and kingdoms.
Although only four papal registers (collections of
important papal letters and decisions) from before
1198 survive more or less intact, all registers since
then have been preserved.

The day-to-day work of the popes was carried out by
the Roman Curia. The Curia consisted of the chancery; the
Apostolic Camera, or financial centre; the consistory, or legal
office, including the Roman Rota (chief papal court); and the
Penitentiary, or spiritual and confessional office. The popes
were also the secular rulers of Rome and the Papal States,

The Palais des Papes (Popes' Palace) in Avignon, France, is one of the oldest châteaux-forts still standing. It was built in two stages: 1334–42 under Benedict XII and 1342–52 under Clement VI.

and accordingly their servants included the rulers and officials of these territories.

The popes ran afoul of local movements for greater independence, including the revolution led by Arnold of Brescia, the priest and religious dissident, in 1143. Revolts continued throughout the 13th century and increased in frequency during the Avignon papacy (1305–78), when the popes resided in Avignon, and during the Great Schism (1378–1417), when there were two and then three claimants for the papal office. (The crisis was resolved in 1415–18 at the Council of Constance, which elected a new pope and restored papal authority over the city of Rome and the Papal States.) When a pope could safely reside in Rome, he worked at the church of St. John Lateran, his cathedral as bishop of the city of Rome, and not at the Vatican, which was chiefly a pilgrimage shrine. Only after Martin V (1417–31), the pope elected at the Council of Constance, found that the papal quarters at the Lateran had fallen into ruins was the papal residence and administration moved to the Vatican.

THE CHURCH HIERARCHY BELOW THE POPE

Lower levels of the clerical hierarchy replicated the papal administration on a smaller scale. The immense dioceses of northern Europe, ruled by prince-archbishops (as in Cologne) or by prince-bishops (as in Durham), were very different from the tiny rural dioceses of southern Italy. Within the secular clergy the highest rank below the pope was that of primate, who was usually the regional head of a group of archbishops. The archbishops, or metropolitans, ruled archdioceses, or provinces, holding provincial synods of clergy under their jurisdiction, ruling administrative courts, and supervising the suffragan bishops (bishops assigned to assist in the administration of the archdiocese). The archbishop was expected to make regular visits to the ecclesiastical institutions in his province and to hear appeals

The Gothic cathedral of Siena, Italy, was built between 1285 and 1377.

from the verdicts of courts at lower levels.

The archdiocese was divided into dioceses, each ruled by a bishop, who supervised his own administration and episcopal court. In ecclesiastical tradition, bishops were considered the successors of the Apostles, and a strong sense of episcopal collegiality between pope and bishops survived well into the age of increased papal authority. Episcopal courts included a chancery for the use of the bishop's seal, a judicial court under the direction of the official or the archdeacon, financial officers, and archpriests (priests assigned to special functions). The bishop's church, the cathedral, was staffed by a chapter (a body of clergy) and headed by a dean, who was specifically charged with administering the cathedral and its property. The chapter was not usually the bishop's administrative staff and thus sometimes found itself in conflict with the bishop. Struggles between bishop and chapter were frequent and notorious in canon law courts, since they could be appealed, like disputed episcopal elections, all the way to the papal court.

Episcopal powers were extensive: only the bishop could consecrate churches, ordain clergy, license preachers, or appoint teachers in episcopal schools. The bishop's pastoral responsibilities extended to all Christians in his diocese. Moreover, since canon law touched the lives of all Christians, episcopal legal officials held great power. They visited diocesan institutions and presided over trials of those accused of violating canon law, which concerned many areas that in modern legal systems are subsumed under civil and criminal law, family courts, and moral offenses.

The diocese was divided into deaconries for the archdeacons, which might convoke lesser synods. Deaconries too had their own chancellors, notaries, and judicial officers, as well as archpriests who assisted the deacons. Since the archdeacon or official was usually the point of contact between the laity and ecclesiastical discipline, they were often the butt of satire and complaint. One topic said to have been proposed for debate at a 13th-century university was: Can an archdeacon be saved?

At the lowest level of the clerical hierarchy was the parish, with its priest, suffragan priests, vicars, and chaplains, who together supervised the spiritual life of the majority of European laity. The parish owned its church and the land that provided the priest's income (the glebe); additional income was derived from tithes collected from all parishioners and often from an endowment.

The priest was presented to the bishop for ordination by a layman, cleric, or clerical corporation with proprietary rights over the parish. In many cases, the actual care of souls in a parish was in the hands of a vicar, who was deputed by a patron to perform the priest's duties when the priest was away studying or occupied in other business. The parish priest also administered the ecclesiastical calendar for his parishioners. Parishioners themselves might belong to spiritual associations, called confraternities, but all were expected to be baptized, to make confession once a year (after the fourth Lateran Council prescribed this in 1215), to take Holy Communion, to marry, and to be buried in the parish churchyard. The parish was the level at which most people learned their Christianity and the level at which most of them lived it.

SCA
VVAL   BVRG
HITDA
ABBA

In the Middle Ages abbesses such as Hilda and Walburga
occasionally ruled double monasteries of monks and nuns and
enjoyed various privileges and honours.

DEVOTIONAL LIFE

The popes also supervised the regular clergy, which included the religious orders of monks, canons regular (secular clergy who lived collegiately according to a rule), and mendicants. Each of these orders had a superior, who was advised by a chapter general that comprised representatives of the religious houses of the order. Orders, like dioceses, were organized according to regions, each having a regional superior and holding regional chapters. Individual religious houses were headed by an abbot or abbess (the mendicant orders had a slightly different organization) and administered by a chancellor and chamberlain. Provosts and deans usually supervised the property of each house.

In the 12th century, new devotional movements (movements devoted to Jesus or the saints) led to outbursts of religious dissent (with new forms of ecclesiastical discipline devised to control them) and equally passionate expressions of orthodox devotion. The most dynamic movement was that of the mendicant orders, the Dominicans and the Franciscans, founded in the early 13th century. The Order of Friars Minor, founded by the layman Francis of Assisi (1181/82–1226) to minister to the spiritual needs of the cities, spread widely and rapidly, as did the Order of Preachers, founded by the canon of Osma, Dominic of Guzmán (c. 1170–1221). These and other devotional movements of laypeople were supported by Pope Innocent III and his successors. The mendicant orders greatly influenced popular piety, because they specialized in preaching in new churches that were built to hold large crowds. Indeed, during this time the sermon came into its own as the most effective mass medium in Europe.

Saint Francis of Assisi's evangelical zeal, consecration to poverty, charity, and personal charisma drew thousands of followers.

The mendicants also increased devotion to the Virgin Mary and to the infant or crucified and suffering Jesus, rather than to the figure of Jesus as regal and remote.

Other forms of devotional life took shape during the 12th, 13th, and 14th centuries. The Cistercian Order, for example, instituted the status of lay brother, who was usually an adult layman who retired from the world to undertake the management of monastic resources. Still other members of the laity retired to the sequestered life of hermits and recluses, usually under the supervision of a chaplain.

During the 13th and 14th centuries, devotional movements arose that were neither monastic nor clerical in any other sense. The most notable of these was the Beguines, an order of devout women (and occasionally, but more rarely, men, who lived in all-male communities and were called Beghards) who lived together in devotional communities within towns, especially in the Low Countries and the Rhineland, followed no rule, and took no vow. They worked in the towns but lived collectively and might leave for marriage or another form of life at any time. Some of the most important devotional literature of the period was written by and for Beguines.

The vast movements of reform, ecclesiastical organization, and pastoral care of the 12th and 13th centuries reached their greatest intensity in the pontificate of Innocent III (1198–1216). Lothar of Segni, as he was originally known, was the son of a landholding noble family outside Rome; he was educated in the schools of Paris and attached to the Roman Curia in 1187. Innocent issued the strongest and most tightly argued claims for papal authority, and he launched Crusades and instituted the office of papal judge-delegate to combat clerical crimes and heterodox belief. He also supported the new mendicant orders, paid particular attention to the needs of popular devotion, reformed and disciplined the Curia, and assembled the fourth Lateran Council in November 1215. Innocent came as close to realizing the ideals of reform and renewal in ecclesiological practice as any pope before or since.

The organization of normative religion, the formal rules and norms of practice in the faith, was intended to give regularity and order to lived religion. Daily religious life was characterized by the acceptance of tradition and authority and by belief in the saints as patrons of local communities and belief in the parish priest as a conveyor of grace by virtue of his sacramental powers (conferred by ordination) and his legal powers (conferred by the bishop). During the 12th century, institutional structures for official acts of canonization were established, but the enthusiasm for the saints remained an important part of both popular devotion and the official cult of the saints (the system of religious belief and ritual surrounding the saints). The cult of the saints was celebrated by clergy and laity in the observance of feast days and processions, the veneration of saints' relics, pilgrimages to saints' shrines, and the rituals of death and burial near the graves of saints. The liturgical dimension of pastoral care regulated the major events of the day, week, season, and Christian year, according to whose rhythms everyone lived. Priests blessed harvests, animals, and ships and liturgically interceded in the face of natural or man-made disasters.

Religious devotion strengthened the presence of normative religion in marriage and the family, the sacred character of the local community and the territorial monarchy, and

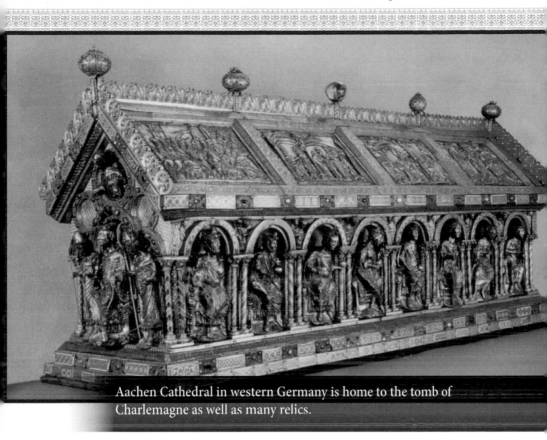

Aachen Cathedral in western Germany is home to the tomb of
Charlemagne as well as many relics.

the moral rules by which lay affairs were conducted. The
fourth Lateran Council largely institutionalized the work of
the 12th-century moral theologians at Paris, who had begun
to apply the principles of doctrine and canon law to the lives
of their contemporaries.

CHRISTIANITY, JUDAISM, AND ISLAM

The sacred texts of revealed religions may be eternal and
unchanging, but they are understood and applied by human
beings living in time. Christians believed not only that
the Jews had misunderstood Scripture, thus justifying the

CRIME AND PUNISHMENT

The ecclesiastical reform movements sharply distinguished clergy from laity. Clergy were not only freed from most forms of subordination to laypersons but also were granted legal privileges, being triable only in church courts and subject only to penalties deemed suitable by church authorities. Laity who injured clerical personnel or property were punished more harshly. But the distinction between clergy and laity also enhanced lay status. Lay authorities could legally perform judicial actions that were forbidden to clergy, like the shedding of blood or other forms of physical punishment. Clerical thinkers greatly legitimated lay activities that earlier monastic Christianity had once scorned, attributing a positive value to commerce, the law, just warfare, marriage, and other roles once considered signs of fallen and weak human nature.

The intensity of the reform movements led to a new and elaborated idea of sin and to categories of sin so grave that they required the harshest punishments, sometimes in cooperation with lay courts. The idea of crime itself, drawing on both older Roman law and earlier ecclesiastical discipline, gradually came to assume a distinctive place in secular law, as more and more conflicts that had once been settled privately came within the purview of lay legal officials. Clerical crime became a major focus of disciplinary concern. The term "heresy," loosely used until the 11th century, slowly became better defined and was initially applied to clerical misconduct. The increasingly precise exposition of Christian doctrine by 12th-century theologians seemed to many people a displacement of the Christianity that they had always understood and practiced. Legal collections began to treat forms of doctrinal and devotional dissent as heresy, thus formulating a category that would criminalize a wide variety of beliefs and conduct.

Promoters of the new ecclesiastical doctrine and discipline believed that the increasingly numerous devotional collectives and their charismatic leaders would eventually threaten the order of both clerical and lay society. In the early 13th century the English theologian Robert Grosseteste formulated a definition that accurately reflected the changed understanding of religious dissent: "Heresy is an opinion chosen by human faculties, contrary to sacred scripture, openly taught, and pertinaciously defended." Criminal heresy involved belief that contradicted orthodox doctrine and was arrived at by purely human capacities.

Like the problem of criminal clergy, the problem of heresy raised

English bishop and scholar Robert Grosseteste introduced into the world of European Christendom Latin translations of Greek and Arabic philosophical and scientific writings.

procedural questions in law. Legal procedure in criminal cases might be initiated by an accusation by a responsible individual or by a denunciation by a group of specially appointed synodal witnesses. In 1199 Innocent III added a third procedure, that of inquisition, or inquiry by an appropriate authority, which was first used to investigate clerical crimes. Later popes appointed judges delegate as individual inquisitors, although there was not an institutionalized office of inquisition until the royal-papal establishment of the Spanish Inquisition in 1478.

Christian reinterpretation of Jewish Scripture, but that all of Jewish Scripture had to be understood as containing only partial truth. The whole truth was comprehensible only when Jewish Scripture was interpreted correctly, in what Christians called a "spiritual" rather than merely a "carnal" manner.

Although early Christian texts and later papal commands had prohibited the persecution and forced conversion of Jews, these doctrines were less carefully observed starting in the 11th century. Heralded by a series of pogroms in both Europe and the Middle East carried out in the course of the First Crusade, a deeper and more widespread anti-Judaism came to characterize much of European history after 1100. There also emerged in this period what some historians have termed "chimeric" anti-Judaism, the conception of the Jew not only as ignorant of spiritual truth and stubbornly resistant to Christian preaching but as actively hostile to Christianity and guilty of ugly crimes against it, such as the ritual murder of Christian children and the desecration of the consecrated host of the mass. This form of anti-Judaism resulted in massacres of Jews, usually at moments of high social tension within Christian communities. One of the best documented of these massacres took place at York, England, in 1190.

Before the 11th century the Jews faced little persecution, lived among Christians, and even pursued the same occupations as Christians. The Jews' restricted status after that time encouraged many of them to turn to moneylending, which only served to increase Christian hostility (Christians were forbidden to lend money to other Christians). Because the Jews often undertook on behalf

This 14th-century miniature depicts the expulsion of Jews from France.

of rulers work that Christians would not do or were not encouraged to do, such as serving as physicians and financial officers, Jews were hated both for their religion and for their social roles.

Jewish identity was also visually marked. Jews were depicted in particular ways in art, and the fourth Lateran Council in 1215 insisted that Jews wear identifying marks on their clothing. Even when not savagely persecuted, Jews were considered the property of the territorial monarchs of Europe and could be routinely exploited economically and even expelled, as they were from England in 1290, France in 1306, and Spain in 1492.

This illuminated page from the *Beatus Apocalypse* is an example of Mozarabic art. Mozarabs were Christians who lived in the Iberian Peninsula after the Arab invasion of 711.

Yet Christians also believed that it was necessary for the Jews to continue to exist unconverted, because the Apocalypse, or Revelation to John, the last book of the Christian Bible, stated that the Jews would be converted at the end of time. Therefore, a "saving remnant" of Jews needed to exist so that scriptural prophecy would be fulfilled.

Muslims, on the other hand, possessed neither the historical status of Jews nor their place in salvation history (the course of events from Creation to the Last Judgment). To many Christian thinkers, Muslims were former Christian heretics who worshipped Muhammad, the Prophet of Islam, and were guilty of occupying the Holy Land and threatening Christendom with military force. The First Crusade had been launched to liberate the Holy Land from Islamic rule, and later Crusades were undertaken to defend the original conquest.

The Crusading movement failed for many reasons but mainly because the Crusaders could not sustain a military and political outpost so far from the heartland of western

Europe. But as a component of European culture, the Crusade ideal remained prominent, even in the 15th and 16th centuries, when the powerful Ottoman Empire indeed threatened to sweep over Mediterranean and southeastern Europe. Not until the Treaty of Carlowitz in 1699 was a stable frontier between the Ottoman Empire and the Holy Roman Empire established.

Contempt for Islam and fear of Muslim military power did not, however, prevent a lively and expansive commercial and technological transfer between the two civilizations or between them and the Byzantine Empire. Commercial and intellectual exchanges between Islamic lands and western Europe were considerable. Muslim maritime, agricultural, and technological innovations, as well as much East Asian technology via the Muslim world, made their way to western Europe in one of the largest technology transfers in world history. What Europeans did not invent they readily borrowed and adapted for their own use. Christian Europe had been well behind the Islamic states and Byzantium in virtually all aspects of material and intellectual culture. By the end of the 13th century it had begun to pull even, and by the end of the 15th century it had surpassed both.

CHAPTER FIVE

FROM TERRITORIAL PRINCIPALITIES TO TERRITORIAL MONARCHIES

As a result of the Investiture Controversy of the late 11th and early 12th centuries, the office of emperor lost much of its religious character and retained only a nominal universal preeminence over other rulers, though several 12th- and 13th-century emperors reasserted their authority on the basis of their interpretation of Roman law and energetically applied their lordship and pursued their dynastic interests in Germany and northern Italy. But the struggle over investiture and the reform movement also legitimized all secular authorities, partly on the grounds of their obligation to enforce discipline. The most successful rulers of the 12th and 13th centuries were, first, individual lords who created compact and more intensely governed principalities and, second and most important, kings who successfully asserted their authority over the princes, often with princely cooperation. The monarchies of

England, France, León-Castile, Aragon, Scandinavia, Portugal, and elsewhere all acquired their fundamental shape and character in the 12th century.

THE OFFICE AND PERSON OF THE KING

By the 12th century, most European political thinkers agreed that monarchy was the ideal form of governance, since it imitated on earth the model set by God for the universe. It was also the form of government of the ancient Hebrews, the Roman Empire, and the peoples who succeeded Rome after the 4th century. For several centuries, some areas had no monarch, but these were regarded as anomalies. Iceland (until its absorption by Norway in 1262) was governed by an association of free men and heads of households meeting in an annual assembly. Many city-republics in northern Italy—especially Florence, Milan, Genoa, Pisa, and Venice—were in effect independent from the 10th to the 16th century, though they were nominally under the rule of the emperor. Elsewhere in Europe, the prosperous and volatile cities of the Low Countries frequently asserted considerable independence from the counts of Flanders and the dukes of Brabant. In the 15th century the forest cantons of Switzerland won effective independence from their episcopal and lay masters. For the rest of Europe, however, monarchy was both a theoretical norm and a factual reality.

Whereas kings were originally rulers of peoples, from the 11th century they gradually became rulers of peoples in geographic territories, and kingdoms came to designate both ruled peoples and the lands they inhabited. Gradually, inventories of royal resources, royal legislation, and the idea

The Allegory of Good and Bad Government (1338–39) by Ambrogio Lorenzetti covers the council room of the Palazzo Pubblico (town hall) of Siena, Italy.

of borders and territorial maps became components of territorial monarchies.

Kings acquired their thrones by inheritance, by election or acclamation (as in the empire), or by conquest. The first two means were considered the most legitimate, unless conquest was carried out at the request or command of a legitimate authority, usually the pope.

The king's position was confirmed by a coronation ceremony, which acknowledged what royal blood claimed: a dynastic right to the throne, borne by a family rather than a designated individual. Inheritance of the throne might involve the successor's being designated coruler while the previous king still lived (as in France), designation by the will of the predecessor, or simply agreement and acclamation by the

COURTS AND ASSEMBLIES

Kings ruled through their courts, which were gradually transformed from private households into elaborate bureaucracies. Royal religious needs were served by royal chapels—whose personnel often became bishops in the kingdom—and by clerical chancellors, who were responsible for issuing and sealing royal documents. Royal chanceries, financial offices, and law courts became specialized institutions during the 12th century. They recruited people of skill as well as of respectable birth, and they established programs to ensure uniformity and norms of professional competence, goals that were increasingly aided by the education offered by the new universities.

In some circumstances, kings were expected to seek and follow the advice of the most important men in their kingdoms, and these gatherings were formalized after the 12th century.

Kings also sometimes convened larger assemblies of lower-ranking subjects in order to issue their commands or urge approval of financial demands. As kings grew stronger and their bureaucracies more articulated, their costs, particularly for war, also increased. Greater financial needs often determined a king's use of representative institutions in order to gain widespread acceptance of new direct or indirect taxation.

These assemblies developed differently in different kingdoms. In England the first Parliaments were held in the late 13th century, though they were not powerful institutions until the 16th century. In France the Parlement developed into a royal law court, while the intermittent meetings of the Estates-General (a representative assembly of the three orders of society) served as an instrument of consultation and communication for the kings. Across Europe these representative assemblies were composed differently, functioned differently, and possessed different degrees of influence on the ruler and the rest of the kingdom. Their later role as essential and powerful components of government began only in the 16th and 17th centuries.

In this miniature from 1040, Holy Roman emperor Henry III is surrounded by objects symbolizing his power.

most important and powerful royal subjects. When dynasties died out in the male line, the search for a ruler became more complicated; if a woman succeeded, there were usually intense debates about the legitimacy of female succession. Liturgical anointing with consecrated oil was accompanied by the ceremonial presentation to the king of objects with symbolic meaning (the crown, the sword of justice, and the helmet, robe, and scepter), by the chanting of prayers dedicated to rulership, and usually by an oath, in which the king swore to protect the church, the weak, and the peace of his kingdom, to administer justice, and to defend the kingdom against its (and his) enemies.

From the very beginning of European history, kings had responsibilities as well as rights and powers. Kings who were thought to have violated their oaths might be considered tyrants or incompetents, and a number of kings were deposed by local factions or papal command, especially in the 13th and 14th centuries. Depositions also required ceremonies that reversed the coronation liturgy.

The territorial monarchies represented something entirely new in world history. Although they often borrowed from the political literature of antiquity—from the Greek philosopher Aristotle, the Roman statesman Cicero, and Roman epic poetry—they applied it to a very different world, one whose ideas were shaped by courtiers, professors, and canon lawyers as well as by political philosophers. Incorporating both clergy and laity under vigorous royal dynasties, the kingdoms of Europe grew out of the political experience of the papacy, the north Italian city-republics, and their own internal development. By the 15th century the territorial monarchies had laid the groundwork for the modern

Philip VI, king of France from 1328 to 1350, presides over judicial proceedings against Robert of Artois.

state. When, to further their own interests, they began to incorporate successively lower levels of society, they also laid the groundwork for the nation. The combination of these, the nation-state, became the characteristic form of the early modern European and Atlantic polity.

THE THREE ORDERS

In the 11th and 12th centuries thinkers argued that human society consisted of three orders: those who fight, those who pray, and those who labour. The structure of the second order, the clergy, was in place by 1200 and remained intact until the religious reformations of the 16th century. The very general category of those who labour (specifically, those who were not knightly warriors or nobles) diversified rapidly after the 11th century into the lively and energetic worlds of peasants, skilled artisans, merchants, financiers, lay professionals, and entrepreneurs, which together drove the European economy to its greatest achievements. The first order, those who fight, was the rank of the politically powerful, ambitious, and dangerous. Kings took pains to ensure that it did not resist their authority.

The term "noble" was originally used to refer to members of kinship groups whose names and heroic past were known, respected, and recognized by others (though it was not usually used by members of such groups themselves). Noble groups married into each other, recognizing the importance of both the female and the male lines. Charlemagne used this international nobility to rule his empire, and its descendants became the nobility of the 11th and 12th centuries, though by then understanding of noble status had

This medieval illustration depicts a shopkeeper, a blacksmith, and two carpenters, representing the diversification of occupations in the later Middle Ages.

changed. During the 11th century, however, some branches of these broad groups began to identify themselves increasingly with the paternal line. They based their identity on their possession of a particular territory handed down from generation to generation, forming patriarchal lineages whose consciousness of themselves differed from that of their predecessors. Titles such as count or duke were originally those of royal service and might increase the prestige and wealth of a family but were not originally essential to noble status. Nor were even kings thought to be able to ennoble someone who was not noble by birth. As the status of the free peasant population was diminished, freedom and unfreedom, as noted above, gradually became the most significant social division.

The new warrior order encompassed both great nobles and lesser fighting men who depended upon the great nobles for support. This assistance usually took the form of land or income drawn from the lord's resources, which could also bring the hope of social advancement, even marriage into a lordly family. The acute need on the part of these lower-ranking warriors was to distinguish themselves from peasants—hence the relegation of all who were not warriors to the vague category of those who labour.

Some nobles asserted their nobility by seizing territory, controlling it and its inhabitants from a castle, surviving as local powers over several generations, marrying well, achieving recognition from their neighbours, and dispensing ecclesiastical patronage to nearby monasteries. The greatest and wealthiest of the nobles controlled vast areas of land, which they received by inheritance or through a grant from the king. Some of them developed closely governed territo-

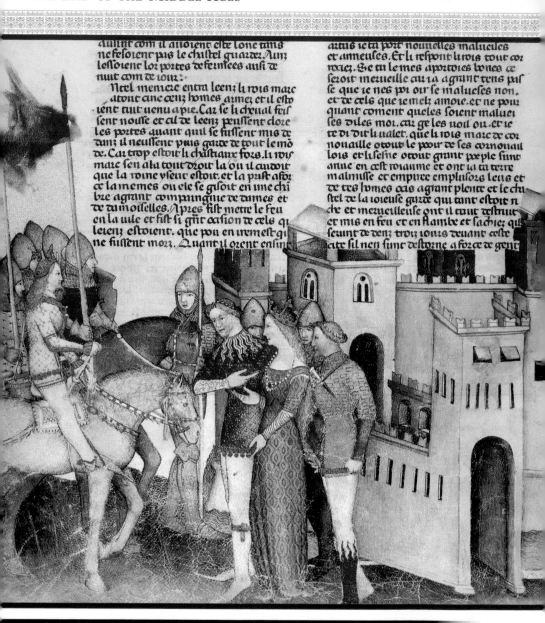

dulint com il auoient elle lone tans
ne fesoient pas le chastel guaittez. Ains
lessoient los portes desermees ansi de
nuit com de iour:·

Itel meniere entra leens li rois mare
atout cinc cenz homes armez et il esto
ient tuit uenu a pie. Car se li cheual feis
sent noise et cil de leens peussent clore
les portes quant quil se fussent mis de
dans il neussent puis garde de tout le mõ
de. Car trop estoit li chastianz fors. li rois
mare sen ala tout droit la ou il cuidoit
que la roine yseut estoit. et la prist afor
ce la memes ou ele se gisoit en une chã
bre agrant compaignie de dames et
de damoiselles. Apres fist mettre le feu
en la uile et fist si grãt ocasion de cels qi
leienz estoient. que poi en iremest qi
ne fussent morz. Quant il orent ensinc

armes se en port nouuelles maluenes
et anueuses. Et li respont li rois tout cou
rociez. Se en le mes aportoies bones ce
seroit merueille cau ia agrant tens pas
se que ie nes poi oir se maluenes non.
et de cels que ie meuz amoie. et ne pour
quant coment queles soient maluei
ses dites moi. car ge ge uoil oir. et en
te di dit li ualet. que li rois mare de cor
nouaille otout le pooir de ses cornouail
lois et lisesne otout grant peple sunt
arriue en cest roiaume et ont ia ca te terre
malmisse et empire emplisore leus et
de tres bones ocis agrant plente et le chã
stel de la ioieuse garte qui tant estoit ri
che et merueilleuse ont il tout destruit
et mis en feu et en flambe et sachiez qil
seuunt de denz trois iours deuant ceste
cite sil nen sunt destorne a force de genz

rial principalities; in France, these were eventually absorbed and redistributed by the crown to members of the royal family or their favourites. Despite the extreme diversity between knights, lesser nobility, and greater nobility, their common warrior-culture, expressed in the literature and ideology of chivalry, served as an effective social bond, excluding all those who did not share it.

As the territorial monarchies gradually increased in both prestige and power, the higher nobility adjusted by accepting more royal offices, titles, and patronage, developing an elaborate vocabulary of noble status, and restricting access to its ranks even though kings could now ennoble whomever they chose. The culture of chivalry served the ambitions of the lower-ranking nobility, but it also reflected the spectrum of different levels of nobility, all subordinated to the ruler. The culture and power of the European aristocracy lasted until the end of the 18th century.

Conclusion

oth ancient and modern historians have often conceived the existence of civilizations and historical periods in terms of the biological stages of human life: birth, development, maturity, and decay. Once the Middle Ages was identified as a distinct historical period, historians in the 15th and 16th centuries began to describe it as enduring in a sequence of stages from youthful vigour to maturity (in the 12th and 13th centuries) and then sinking into old age (in the 14th and 15th centuries). Much of the evidence used to support this view was based on the series of apparently great disasters that struck Europe in the 14th century: the Mongol invasions, the great famine of 1315, the Black Death of 1348 and subsequent years, the financial collapse of the great Italian banking houses in the early 14th century, and the vastly increased costs and devastating effects of larger-scale warfare. For a long time historians considered these disasters dramatic signs of the end of an age.

Reconsideration of the Europe of the 14th and 15th centuries, however, does not reveal decline or decay but rather a remarkable resilience that enabled it to recover from disaster and reconstitute itself by means of most of the same institutions it had possessed in 1300. The process of rural and urban expansion and development indeed paused in the 14th century as famine, epidemic disease, intensified and prolonged warfare, and financial collapse brought growth to a halt and reduced the population for a time to about half of the 70 million people who had inhabited Europe in 1300. But the resources that had created the Europe of the 12th and 13th centuries survived these crises: first the European countryside and then the cities were rapidly repopulated. That recovery continued through the 16th and 17th centuries.

The missionary mandate reached out across Mongol-dominated Asia as far east as China, where a Christian bishop took up his seat in 1307. Improved techniques in both navigation and marine engineering led Europeans from the 13th century to cross and map first their local seas, then the west African coasts, then the Atlantic and Pacific. From the late 15th century Europe began to export itself once more, as it once had to the north and east from the 10th to the 15th century, this time over vast oceans and to continents that had been unknown to the Greeks and Romans.

Neither the crises of the 14th century nor the voyages and discoveries of the 15th suggest the end of a historical period. Rather, they represent the continued strength and resiliency of a European society and culture that men and women had shaped from the 8th century.

Glossary

ABBOT The superior of an abbey for men.

ARIANISM A theological movement initiated by Arius that held that Jesus, as the son of God, was created by God. It won strong support during the 4th century BCE chiefly in the Eastern churches, but it was condemned in general councils at Nicaea (325 CE) and Constantinople (381 CE).

BISHOP A member of the clergy in the Anglican, Eastern Orthodox, or Roman Catholic churches that ranks above a priest, has authority to ordain and confirm, and typically governs a diocese.

CALIPH A Muslim political leader claiming rightful succession to the caliphate.

CANON A decree, decision, regulation, code, or constitution made by ecclesiastical authority; specifically, a law or rule of doctrine or discipline enacted by a council and confirmed by highest ecclesiastical authority.

CHANCERY The office in which the business of a diocese is transacted and recorded.

CLERICAL Of, relating to, or characteristic of the clergy, the body of men and women duly ordained to the service of God in the Christian church.

CONFESSIONAL Adhering to, established on, or defined by a confession of faith.

DEVOTIONAL Related to earnestness and zeal in the performance of religious duties and observations.

DIALECTIC The theory and practice of weighing and reconciling juxtaposed or contradictory arguments for the purpose of arriving at truth, especially through discussion and debate.

DYNASTIC Of or belonging to a dynasty, a succession of rulers of the same line of descent.

ECCLESIASTICAL Of or relating to a church especially as a formal and established institution.

EPISCOPAL Of, being, or suited to a bishop.

ESCHATOLOGICAL Of, relating to, or dealing with the end of the world or the ultimate destiny of humankind.

FRANK A member of a Germanic-speaking people who invaded the western Roman Empire in the 5th century.

HERESY (HETERODOXY) Adherence to a religious opinion that is contrary to an established dogma of a church.

LAITY The great body of the people of a religious faith as distinguished from its clergy.

LITURGY A rite or series of rites, observances, or procedures prescribed for public worship in the Christian church in accordance with authorized or standard form.

MENDICANT ORDER Any of various religious orders (as the Franciscans, Dominicans, Carmelites, or Augustinians) in which monastic life and outside religious activity are combined and in which neither personal nor community tenure of property is allowed under original regulations.

MONASTIC Of, relating to, or connected with a monastery, a house of religious retirement or of seclusion from the world for persons under religious vows.

ORTHODOX Conforming to the Christian faith as formulated in the church creeds and confessions.

SCHISM A formal division or separation in the Christian church or from a church or religious body.

SERF A person belonging to any of various grades of the lower class especially in different feudal systems, bound to the soil and more or less subject to the will of the owner of the soil, and separable from the lord's land by emancipation only.

SYNOD A formal meeting to consult and decide on church matters.

TRANSALPINE Of, relating to, or situated on the farther side of the Alps.

VISIGOTHS A member of the western division of the Goths that invaded the Roman empire beginning in the 4th century and later established kingdoms between the Loire and Gibraltar.

Bibliography

EUROPE IN THE MIDDLE AGES

Useful reference works are *The New Cambridge Medieval History*, 7 vol. (1995–2005); *Dictionary of the Middle Ages*, 13 vol. (1982–89); and *Encyclopedia of the Middle Ages*, 2 vol. (2000). A good outline of events in the Middle Ages is R.L. Storey, *Chronology of the Medieval World*, 800–1491 (1973). Biographies of some important historians can be found in Helen Damico and Joseph Zavadil (eds.), *Medieval Scholarship: Biographical Studies in the Formation of a Discipline*, 3 vol. (1995–99). Two important volumes that represent scholarly perspectives of the late 20th and early 21st century are Peter Linehan and Janet L. Nelson, *The Medieval World* (2001); and Lester K. Little and Barbara Rosenwein (eds.), *Debating the Middle Ages: Issues and Readings* (1998).

Terminology and periodization are discussed in Fred C. Robinson, "Medieval, the Middle Ages," *Speculum*, 59(4):745–756 (October 1984); William A. Green, "Periodization in European and World History," *Journal of World History*, 3(1):13–53 (Spring 1992); Donald R. Kelley, *Foundations of Modern Historical Scholarship: Language, Law, and History in the French Renaissance* (1970); Lionel Gossman, *Medievalism and the Ideologies of the Enlightenment: The World and Work of La Curne de Sainte-Palaye* (1968); Jacques Le Goff, "The Several Middle Ages of Jules Michelet," in his *Time, Work, and Culture in the Middle Ages* (1980), pp. 3–28; Jacques Heers, *Le Moyen Âge, une imposture* (1992); Timothy Reuter, "Medieval: Another Tyrannous Construct?," *The Medieval History Journal*, 1(1):25–45 (1998), and other articles in the same number. Stuart Airlie, "Strange Eventful Histories: The Middle Ages in the Cinema," chapter 10 in Peter Linehan and Janet L. Nelson, *The*

Medieval World (2001), pp. 163–183, provides an introduction to depictions of the Middle Ages in film.

Discussions of the "long Middle Ages" include Dietrich Gerhard, *Old Europe: A Study of Continuity, 1000–1800* (1981); Jacques Le Goff, "For an Extended Middle Ages," in his *The Medieval Imagination* (1988; originally published in French), pp. 18–23; Howard Kaminsky, "From Lateness to Waning to Crisis: The Burden of the Later Middle Ages," *Journal of Early Modern History*, 4(1):85–125 (November 2000); Elizabeth R. Brown, "On 1500," chapter 29 in Linehan and Nelson's *The Medieval World* (above), pp. 691–710.

Surveys (cited here in reverse chronological sequence) include David Nicholas, *The Transformation of Europe 1300–1600* (1999); R.N. Swanson, *Religion and Devotion in Europe, c. 1215–c. 1515* (1995); Thomas A. Brady, Heiko A. Oberman, and James D. Tracy (eds.), *Handbook of European History, 1400–1600: Late Middle Ages, Renaissance, and Reformation*, 2 vol. (1994–95); Robert Bartlett, *The Making of Europe: Conquest, Colonization, and Cultural Change, 950–1350* (1993); Joseph H. Lynch, *The Medieval Church* (1992); Patrick J. Geary, *Before France and Germany: The Creation and Transformation of the Merovingian World* (1988); J.H. Burns (ed.), *The Cambridge History of Medieval Political Thought, c. 350–c. 1450* (1988; reissued 1997); Brian Tierney, *Religion, Law, and the Growth of Constitutional Thought, 1150–1650* (1982); Francis Oakley, *The Western Church in the Later Middle Ages* (1979, reissued 1987); and R.W. Southern, *The Making of the Middle Ages* (1953, reissued 1998).

The classic work describing the older idea of decay is that of Johan Huizinga, *The Autumn of the Middle Ages*(1996). A useful counterpoint is Kaminsky's "From Lateness to Waning to Crisis" (above).

THE CAROLINGIAN DYNASTY

Basic to any serious study of Charlemagne is Wolfgang Braunfels (ed.), *Karl der Grosse: Lebenswerk und Nachleben*, 3rd ed., 5 vol. (1967–68), a massive collection of essays treating various aspects of his career and policy, each written by a leading authority. Although not easy to use, a rich storehouse of information on Charlemagne is provided in the articles in Rosamond McKittrick (ed.), *The New Cambridge Medieval History* (1995–); the work also has an extensive, up-to-date bibliography. A good treatment of daily life in the age of Charlemagne is Pierre Riché, *Daily Life in the World of Charlemagne*, with expanded footnotes, trans. from the French by Jo Ann McNamara (1978; reissued 1988). Siegfried Epperlein, *Leben am Hofe Karls des Grossen* (2000), provides an engaging description of court life. Charlemagne's system of government is the subject of two collections of studies by one of the most important Carolingian scholars of recent times: François L. Ganshof, *Frankish Institutions under Charles the Great*, trans. by Bryce and Mary Lyon (1968); and François L. Ganshof, *The Carolingians and the Frankish Monarchy. Studies in Carolingian History*, trans. by Janet Sondheimer (1971).

Charlemagne's role in religious life is clearly described in Émile Amann, *L'Époque carolingienne: Histoire de l'Église depuis les origines jusqu'à nos jours*, vol. 6, ed. by Augustin Fliche and Victor Martin (1947), pp. 49–200. Although written from a papal perspective, Thomas F.X. Noble, *The Republic of St. Peter: The Birth of the Papal State, 680–825* (1984), is invaluable in understanding Charlemagne's relationship with the papacy. Economic and social conditions during Charlemagne's reign are treated in Renée Doehaerd, *The Early Middle Ages in the*

West: Economy and Society, trans. by W.G. Deakin (1978, originally published in French, 2nd ed., 1971).

Provocative remarks on the nature of the Carolingian Renaissance are given by John J. Contreni, "The Carolingian Renaissance," in John J. Contreni, *Carolingian Learning, Masters, and Manuscripts* (1992), chapter 3; and Janet L. Nelson, "On the Limits of the Carolingian Renaissance," in Janet L. Nelson, *Politics and Ritual in Early Medieval Europe* (1996), pp. 49–67. Still the best study on the Carolingian Renaissance is Erna Patzelt, *Die karolingische Renaissance* (1965). A provocative treatment of the imperial coronation of 800 is Robert Folz, *The Coronation of Charlemagne, 25 December 800*, trans. by J.E. Anderson (1974; originally published in French, 1964). Rich in insights into the import of the imperial title in the Carolingian world is Louis Halphen, *Charlemagne and the Carolingian Empire*, trans. by Giselle de Nie (1977; originally published in French, 1947, reprinted with updated bibliography, 1995).

CHRISTIANITY IN THE MIDDLE AGES

The church in the Middle Ages is treated in Peter R.L. Brown, *The Rise of Western Christendom: Triumph and Diversity, ad 200–1000*, 2nd ed. (2003); John Bossy, *Christianity in the West, 1400–1700* (1985); Joseph H. Lynch, *The Medieval Church: A Brief History* (1995); Steven Ozment, *The Age of Reform (1250–1550): An Intellectual and Religious History of Late Medieval and Reformation Europe* (1980); and J.M. Wallace-Hadrill, *The Frankish Church* (1983).H.E.W. Turner, *The Pattern of Christian Truth* (1954, reissued 2004), investigates orthodoxy and heresy in the early church. Christian philosophy in the Middle Ages is discussed in Étienne Gilson, *Reason and Revelation in the Middle*

Ages (1938, reprinted 1966), and *History of Christian Philosophy in the Middle Ages* (1955, reissued 1980).

Important issues in medieval Christianity are treated in Jeffrey Burton Russell, *Dissent and Order in the Middle Ages* (1992); and Per Erik Persson, *Sacra Doctrina: Reason and Revelation in Aquinas* (1970; originally published in Swedish, 1957). Works on various aspects of church doctrine include, on the church, Hans Küng, *The Church* (1967, reissued 1976; originally published in German, 1967); on the formation of the biblical canon, Bruce M. Metzger, *The Canon of the New Testament: Its Origin, Development, and Significance* (1987, reissued 1997); on Christian creeds and confessions, Philip Schaff, *Biblioteca Symbolica Ecclesiae Universalis: The Creeds of Christendom*, 6th ed., 3 vol. (1919, reissued 1977); and Jaroslav Pelikan and Valerie R. Hotchkiss, *Creeds and Confessions of Faith in the Christian Tradition*, 4 vol. (2003); on the liturgy, Frank C. Senn, *Christian Liturgy: Catholic and Evangelical* (1997); and James F. White, *Introduction to Christian Worship*, 3rd ed. rev. and expanded (2000); on monasticism, David Knowles, *Christian Monasticism* (1969, reissued 1977); and Jean Leclercq, *The Love of Learning and the Desire for God: A Study of Monastic Culture*, trans. by Catharine Misrahi, 3rd ed. (1982, reissued 2000; originally published in French 1957); and, on Christian art and iconography, Emile Mâle, *Religious Art from the Twelfth to the Eighteenth Century* (1949, reissued 1982; originally published in French, 1945); Leonid Ouspensky and Vladimir Lossky, *The Meaning of Icons*, trans. by G.E.H. Palmer, 2nd ed. (1982; originally published in German, 1952); and Robert Milburn, *Early Christian Art and Architecture* (1988).

Index

A

Aachen, 16
Abelard, Peter, 55
Adhémar of Le Puy, 43, 48
adoptionism, 15–16
agricultural growth, 25, 27, 54
Alaric, 10
Alcuin, 14
Alexius, 42, 45, 47
Alfred, 14, 22
Antioch, 46–47, 48
Arianism, 16
Arnulfing-Pippinid family, 13

B

Baldwin of Le Bourcq, 43
banal jurisdiction, 27
bannum, 27
Bede, 14
Beguines, 71
Bohemond, 43, 45, 47, 48
Boniface, 14

C

canon law, 14, 40, 55, 59, 60, 66,
    73, 85
Capet, Hugh, 20
Carolingian dynasty, 13, 25, 34,
    38
    Carolingian Renaissance,
        14–18,
    decline, 20, 22
celibacy, as requirement of clergy,
    38–39
Charlemagne, 13, 20, 87
    and expansion of territory,

14–18
    legacy, 18–19
Childeric, 12
chivalry, 29, 91
Cistercian Order, 71
Clement II, Pope, 39
clerical crimes, 72, 74–75
clerical hierarchy, structure of, 40,
    64, 66–67, 69
Clermont, Council of, 41
Clovis, 12, 13
Cluny monastery, 23
conciliarism
Concordat of Worms, 61
Concordia discordantium canonum
        ("Concordance of Discor-
        dant Canons"), 55
Conrad I, 20
contado, 36
Corpus Juris Civilis ("Body of Civil
        Law"), 55
correctio, 14
courts and assemblies, monarchi-
        cal rule by, 83
Crusades, 41, 46–48, 76, 78
    leadership of, 43, 45
    preparation for First, 42–43,
        45
    siege of Jerusalem, 40, 49–52

D

deforestation, 31
devotional movements, 69, 71–73
dialectic, 55
Dicuil, 14
Didascalicon, 55
Dominican Order, 69